AMERICA'S GREATEST TEAMS

THE SAN FRANCISCO 49ERS

Sloan MacRae

I0807016

PowerKiDS press

New York

Published in 2011 by The Rosen Publishing Group, Inc.
29 East 21st Street, New York, NY 10010

First Edition

Editor: Amelie von Zumbusch
Book Design: Greg Tucker
Layout Design: Julio Gil

Photo Credits: Cover (Joe Montana), p. 5 Al Messerschmidt/Getty Images; cover (Patrick Willis), pp. 7, 21 Michael Zagaris/Getty Images; cover (Jerry Rice), p. 17 David Madison/Getty Images; cover (background), p. 9 Scott Boehm/Getty Images; p. 11 Frank Rippon/Getty Images; pp. 13, 22 (bottom) Focus on Sport/Getty Images; p. 15 Andy Hayt/Getty Images; p. 19 David Stock/Getty Images; p. 22 (top) Bruce Bennett Studios/Getty Images.

Library of Congress Cataloging-in-Publication Data

MacRae, Sloan.
The San Francisco 49ers / by Sloan MacRae. — 1st ed.
p. cm. — (America's greatest teams)
Includes index.
ISBN 978-1-4488-3166-1 (library binding) — ISBN 978-1-4488-3170-8 (pbk.) —
ISBN 978-1-4488-3171-5 (6-pack)
1. San Francisco 49ers (Football team) I. Title.
GV956.S3M36 2011
796.332'640979461—dc22
2010036274

Manufactured in the United States of America

CPSIA Compliance Information: Batch #WW11PK: For Further Information contact Rosen Publishing, New York, New York at 1-800-237-9932

CONTENTS

FIVE SUPER BOWLS

Some football teams never win a **Super Bowl**. Many win only one or two. The San Francisco 49ers won five Super Bowls in a very short time. Few other **professional** football teams have had this kind of success.

The 49ers are a young team compared with some other teams in the National Football **League**, or the NFL. Most of the great football teams have been around for a lot longer. They have had more time to win **championships**. The 49ers made NFL history in just a few years. They broke many records. Their players and **coaches** changed the way the game is played.

The 49ers won their fourth Super Bowl in 1990. Joe Montana (center) was named the game's most valuable player, or MVP, for a record-breaking third time.

GOLD RUSH

The 49ers play in San Francisco, California. The state of California is known for the famous **gold rush** of 1849. Many people moved there then to look for gold. They were called 49ers. The people of California are proud of this period of American history. This is where the San Francisco 49ers get their name. Gold is even one of the team's colors. The other colors are red and white.

All NFL teams have special signs called **logos**. The 49ers logo shows the letters *S* and *F*. They stand for "San Francisco." Some fans also call the team the Niners.

49ers player Patrick Willis is wearing the team's uniform in this picture. You can see the 49ers' logo on his helmet.

CANDLESTICK PARK

The 49ers play in a **stadium** called Candlestick Park. The stadium is along San Francisco Bay. It is one of the most famous stadiums in the world. This is not just because of the 49ers, though. Candlestick Park also used to be the home of San Francisco's baseball team, the Giants.

The rock band the Beatles played their last show ever there. Many people believe the Beatles are the greatest band of all time. This means some of the best football players, baseball players, and rock musicians in history have played at Candlestick Park. Fans at Candlestick Park have been very lucky!

Candlestick Park sits on a point of land called Candlestick Point. Fans voted to pick the stadium's name in 1959. The stadium opened the next year.

CALIFORNIA FOOTBALL

California was not known for its football in the early days of the game. The sport had taken off in cities like New York and Chicago. There was no professional football team in California. A businessman and football fan named Tony Morabito knew that football could be a hit in San Francisco, though. There were several California colleges with great football teams.

Morabito worked hard to bring a football team to San Francisco during the early 1940s. The 49ers took the field in 1946. They joined the NFL in 1950. The 49ers were a good team in the 1950s. They were not quite ready to make history, though.

Joe Perry (left) and Y. A. Tittle (second from left) were stars for the 49ers in the 1950s. They are now both in the Pro Football Hall of Fame.

THE SHOTGUN FORMATION

The 49ers changed the game of football in the 1960s. Coach Red Hickey used a plan called the shotgun formation. In the shotgun formation, the **quarterback** stands farther back than quarterbacks generally do when the ball is **snapped**. This lets him have more time to throw the ball before the other team's **defense** can reach him.

San Francisco quarterback John Brodie played very well in the shotgun formation. The plan caught on quickly. Soon, other teams started to use it. The 49ers beat some very good teams in the 1960s and 1970s. However, they were not yet on top of the NFL.

John Brodie (center) played for the 49ers between 1957 and 1973. He was born in San Francisco and grew up in nearby Oakland, California.

BILL WALSH AND THE WEST COAST OFFENSE

In 1979, the 49ers hired a new coach named Bill Walsh. Walsh soon proved himself to be one of the smartest coaches in the NFL. He was one of the first coaches to use what is now called the West Coast **offense**. The 49ers had already changed football with the shotgun formation. The West Coast offense changed the game again. It lets the quarterback move the ball down the field with short, quick passes.

Quarterback Joe Montana quickly became one of the best football players in history by using the West Coast offense. In 1982, he and the 49ers won their first Super Bowl against the Cincinnati Bengals.

Walsh (left) said of Montana (right), "The minute I saw Joe move, there was no question in my mind that he was the best I'd seen."

THE TEAM OF THE 80S

The 49ers reached the Super Bowl again in 1985. This time they faced the Miami Dolphins. The Dolphins had a great quarterback named Dan Marino. Montana and the 49ers won, though.

In 1985, San Francisco **drafted** a talented **wide receiver** named Jerry Rice. The great quarterback now had a great receiver to catch his passes. The 49ers won a third Super Bowl in 1989. It was a very close game against the Bengals. San Francisco returned to the Super Bowl the next year. They crushed the Denver Broncos. Montana became just the second NFL quarterback to win four Super Bowls. Football fans called the 49ers the Team of the 80s.

Rice played for the 49ers through the 2000 season. By the time he stopped playing, in 2004, Rice had made 208 touchdowns!

STEVE YOUNG

The 49ers were now a football **dynasty**. They had won four Super Bowls in just a few seasons. They were the best team in the NFL. San Francisco was not finished winning Super Bowls, though.

A new quarterback named Steve Young took over in the early 1990s. Young led the 49ers to their fifth Super Bowl in 1995. No NFL team had won five Super Bowls at this time. San Francisco faced the San Diego Chargers. This was the first time two California teams had played in the Super Bowl. Young and the 49ers won a record-breaking fifth NFL championship for the city of San Francisco.

Young led the NFL in passing in six different years. Only one other player had ever led the NFL in passing this many times.

A NEW DYNASTY IN THE MAKING

No team stays on top of the NFL forever. The 49ers began to struggle in the 2000s. They still had great players. However, they could not put a championship team together. San Francisco fans know that their team has already made NFL history and has changed the game forever. Most NFL teams can only dream of the level of success San Francisco had in the 1980s and 1990s.

Today, the 49ers have a great coach in Mike Singletary. Singletary won a Super Bowl playing for the Chicago Bears in the 1980s. San Francisco fans hope he will win some as a coach for the 49ers.

Here, Singletary is talking to members of the 49ers offense during a 2009 game against the Jacksonville Jaguars. The 49ers won the game, 20–3.

SAN FRANCISCO 49ERS TIMELINE

1946

The 49ers play their first game. They beat the Chicago Rockets.

1950

The 49ers play their first game in the NFL. They lose to the New York Yanks.

1960

The 49ers' coach Red Hickey confuses the Baltimore Colts with the shotgun formation.

1979

The 49ers draft quarterback Joe Montana.

1982

On January 10, Dwight Clark makes a great catch on a pass from Joe Montana. This play is now so famous that it is known as the Catch.

1982

The 49ers win their first Super Bowl by beating the Cincinnati Bengals on January 24.

1990

The 49ers win their fourth Super Bowl. Montana becomes the second quarterback ever to win four Super Bowls.

1995

Steve Young leads the 49ers to become the first NFL team to win five Super Bowls.

2008

Mike Singletary becomes head coach of the 49ers.

GLOSSARY

CHAMPIONSHIPS (CHAM-pee-un-ships) Games held to decide the best, or the winner.

COACHES (KOHCH-ez) People who direct teams.

DEFENSE (DEE-fents) When a team tries to stop the other team from scoring.

DRAFTED (DRAFT-ed) Picked for a special purpose.

DYNASTY (DY-nas-tee) A powerful group that keeps its position for a long time.

GOLD RUSH (GOHLD RUSH) A time in history when people found gold in the ground.

LEAGUE (LEEG) A group of sports teams.

LOGOS (LOH-gohz) Pictures, words, or letters that stand for teams or companies.

OFFENSE (O-fents) When a team tries to score points in a game.

PROFESSIONAL (pruh-FESH-nul) Having players who are paid.

QUARTERBACK (KWAHR-ter-bak) A football player who directs the team's plays.

SNAPPED (SNAPD) Handed or thrown to a member of a football team's offense.

STADIUM (STAY-dee-um) A place where sports are played.

SUPER BOWL (SOO-per BOHL) The championship game of NFL football.

WIDE RECEIVER (WYD rih-SEE-ver) A football player whose biggest job is to catch passes from the quarterback.

INDEX

WEB SITES

Due to the changing nature of Internet links, PowerKids Press has developed an online list of Web sites related to the subject of this book. This site is updated regularly. Please use this link to access the list:
www.powerkidslinks.com/teams/fsanfran/